SOME IMPORTANT PLACES IN CLAUDE MONET'S LIFE

1. **Paris, France.** Claude Monet was born in the capital city of France in 1840.

2. **Le Havre, France.** When Claude was five years old, his family moved to this busy seaport town.

3. **London, England.** As a young man, Claude lived in London for a while. Years later he would return to paint scenes of the city.

4. **Argenteuil, France.** Monet and his family lived in this picturesque village in the 1870s. He painted some of his most famous works there.

5. **Etretat, France.** This rocky, seaside area was a favorite painting spot for Monet.

6. **Giverny, France.** Claude Monet bought a house in this small village and created his famous garden there.

7. **The French Riviera and the Italian Riviera.** These seaside areas were popular spots for impressionist artists, including Monet and his friend Pierre Auguste Renoir.

8. **Venice, Italy.** Monet traveled here when he was 68. Venice is famous for having canals instead of streets. Monet's paintings perfectly captured the misty weather and ancient buildings reflected in Venice's canals.

THIS IS THE AREA THAT'S SHOWN ON THE LARGER MAP

MAP OF THE ENTIRE TOTAL COMPLETE WORLD

IRELAND

ENGLAND

London ⭐ **3**

ENGLISH CHANNEL

NETHERLANDS

GERMANY

BELGIUM

ATLANTIC OCEAN

1
Paris ⭐

FRANCE

SWITZERLAND

AUSTRIA

SLOVENIA

Venice

8

ADRIATIC SEA

PORTUGAL

SPAIN

7
The French Riviera AND The Italian Riviera

ITALY

2 Le Havre

5 Etretat

SEINE RIVER

6 Giverny

● Argenteuil

4

MEDITERRANEAN SEA

This map is a closer look at the area of France outlined above.

Paris ⭐

TIMELINE OF CLAUDE MONET'S LIFE

1840 Claude Monet is born in Paris.

1845 The Monet family moves to the seaport city of Le Havre.

1858 Local landscape artist Eugène Boudin convinces Claude to try painting outdoors, something that wasn't being done very often back then.

1862 Claude Monet travels to Paris to study art. There he makes friends with many soon-to-be famous artists.

1865 Monet is excited to have two of his paintings accepted by the important Paris Salon.

1870 Monet makes his first trip to London.

1871-1878 Monet paints tons of impressionist scenes in Argenteuil.

1874 Claude helps organize the first impressionist exhibition. The term *impressionism* comes from the title of a painting he enters, *Impression Sunrise.*

THIS WAY

1882 Monet paints the first of many scenes of the rocky ocean cliffs at Etretat.

1883 Claude Monet moves to Giverny. He builds a large water garden there with a Japanese footbridge.

1884 Monet travels to the Italian Riviera and paints scenes along the sunny coast.

1888 Monet visits the French Riviera.

1890 Monet begins his series of grain and haystack paintings.

1899-1901 Monet creates many of his Water Lily paintings.

1908 Monet travels to Venice.

1913 Claude Monet starts painting huge scenes of his garden.

1923 Monet has eye surgery to keep from going blind. A few months later he is able to get back to work.

UP HERE

1926 Monet dies at Giverny.

GETTING TO KNOW THE WORLD'S GREATEST ARTISTS

C L A U D E
MONET

WRITTEN AND ILLUSTRATED BY MIKE VENEZIA

CONSULTANT SARA MOLLMAN UNDERHILL

CHILDREN'S PRESS®

An Imprint of Scholastic Inc.

New York Toronto London Auckland Sydney
Mexico City New Delhi Hong Kong
Danbury, Connecticut

For Sam Freifeld
Thanks for your ideas and encouragement

Cover: *Argenteuil*, 1875.
© Alfredo Dagli Orti/The Art Archive at Art Resource, NY

Library of Congress Cataloging-in-Publication Data

Venezia, Mike, author, illustrator.
[Monet]
 Claude Monet / by Mike Venezia.—Revised Edition.
    pages cm.—(Getting to know the world's greatest artists)
 Includes index.
 ISBN 978-0-531-21979-9 (library binding)—
 ISBN 978-0-531-22540-0 (pbk.)
 1. Monet, Claude, 1840–1926—Juvenile literature. I. Title.

ND553.M7V46 2014
759.4—dc23
[B]   2014014724

©2015 by Mike Venezia Inc.

All rights reserved. Published in 2015 by Children's Press, an imprint of Scholastic Inc. Printed in China 62

1 2 3 4 5 6 7 8 9 10 R 24 23 22 21 20 19 18 17 16 15

Monet Painting in his Garden at Argenteuil, 1873.
By Pierre-Auguste Renoir, Wadsworth Atheneum, Hartford, Connecticut.

Claude Monet was born in Paris,
France, in 1840. He was a great artist
and helped invent an important style
of painting called impressionism.

Many of Monet's paintings are pictures of water. Boats, oceans, ponds, and lakes were some of his favorite subjects.

Terrace at Sainte-Adresse.
The Metropolitan Museum of Art, New York

The Houses of Parliament, Sunset. 1903.
The National Gallery of Art, Washington, D.C.

Claude Monet loved the way colors
reflect in water, and the special
way that water makes the clouds and
sky look.

Monet Working in His Floating Studio Argenteuil by *Manet*
Neue Pinakothek, Munich. Scala/Art Resource

Monet even fixed up a boat as a
floating studio. He kept paints, brushes,
canvas, and drawing supplies on it.
Monet sailed up and down rivers and
streams, stopping to paint wherever
he liked. It must have been fun.

When Claude Monet was little, his
family moved from Paris to the town
of Le Havre, which was right on the
sea. At Le Havre, ships from all over
the world stopped to pick up supplies

for their long journeys. Monet's father
owned a grocery store that sold
supplies to the sailors and shipping
companies. Claude must have seen
a lot of very interesting people while
he was growing up.

Claude Monet had a good sense of humor, but he didn't do very well in school. He never listened to anybody, and spent most of his time drawing funny pictures. He even drew funny pictures of his teachers!

(above) *Mario Uchard*, The Art Institute of Chicago.

(top right) *Léon Manchon, Lawyer,* 1885. The Art Institute of Chicago.

(bottom right) *Caricature of a Man* with a Large Nose. 1855.
The Art Institute of Chicago.

Claude became very good at
drawing these pictures. When he
was a teenager, some people (who also
had a good sense of humor) paid him
to draw pictures of them.

Claude liked making money by selling his drawings. He kept on drawing until a well-known local artist convinced Claude he should try painting.

Eugène Boudin had some new and interesting ideas about painting that Monet liked.

Boudin thought artists should paint
outside, not in stuffy studios like
most artists did during Monet's time.

La Grenouillère, 1869. The Metropolitan Museum of Art, New York

Monet loved the idea of painting outdoors. In 1862, he left Le Havre to study art in Paris. There he met other artists. Monet made friends with Pierre-Auguste Renoir, Alfred Sisely, and Frédéric Bazille. He showed them how much fun it was to paint outdoors. Monet and his friends often painted together in the countryside.

After the invention of oil paint in tubes, it was easier for artists to carry their supplies around and paint outside. Before that, artists had to mix their own paint in jars with colored powder and oil. It was a messy job. There were some problems with painting outside, though. Sometimes sand and other things stuck to the wet paint.

Monet wanted his paintings to become well known so that people would buy them. Almost the only way he could do this was by having his paintings shown at the great Salon in Paris. The Salon was a place where people came from all over the world to see what the best artists were doing.

It wasn't easy to get a painting into the Salon. The few judges picked only the paintings they liked. Monet entered his paintings often. Sometimes they were accepted and sometimes they weren't.

Women in the Garden was one of Monet's paintings that didn't make it.

Women in the Garden, 1867.
Louvre, Paris.
Art Resource/Giraudon

Monet used his favorite model for all four women in this painting. Her name was Camille. Claude Monet and Camille fell in love and got married a few years after this painting was finished.

The Cradle. Camille with Jean, 1867. National Gallery of Art, Washington, D.C.

Monet often used Camille and their children as models. This is a painting of Camille and their first son, Jean.

The great Salon wasn't paying much attention to Monet and his friends, so they decided to have their own show. They wanted people to see how exciting their colorful outdoor paintings were. But the show didn't work out very well.

The Lion Hunt, by Delacroix, 1861. The Art Institute of Chicago

People in Paris in those days wanted to see paintings that told a story about some important battle or historical event. They were used to paintings where everything looked clear and sharp, and they liked dark, moody colors, like the colors in the painting above.

Impression: Sunrise, 1872. Musée Marmottan, Paris. Art Resource

Monet and his friends were more interested in how pretty something looked when the sunlight was on it. They liked to paint ordinary things, like a boat on a lake, or rocks by the ocean, or even haystacks in a field.

A newspaperman called these artists ''impressionists.'' He got the name from Monet's painting *Impression: Sunrise.*

Even though people were not crazy about Monet's impressionist pictures, he kept on painting them. He thought it was important to show scenes of everyday life, and he tried to make the colors, shadows, and light in his paintings as real as possible. Monet was even able to show steam and dampness coming from a train engine.

Gare Saint-Lazare, 1877.
The Art Institute of Chicago

Detail of painting on Page 25

If you take a very close look at some of Monet's paintings, you can hardly tell what he painted. It just looks like a bunch of colorful brush strokes.

The Cliff Walk Pourville, 1882. The Art Institute of Chicago

But when you step back a little, it all starts to make sense. It's easy to see that the colorful brush strokes on page 24 are really the two ladies walking along a cliff in the painting above.

The Manneporte, Etretat, 1883,
The Metropolitan Museum of Art, New York

The exciting brush strokes and colors in Monet's paintings give you the feeling of being right there at the moment he made the painting.

Monet wanted to get as close as he could to the things he was painting, no matter what the conditions were. Sometimes he had to tie his easel down so that the waves wouldn't wash his painting away!

Monet often painted many pictures of the same thing. He wanted to see how sunlight changed the look of something at different times of the day, or at different seasons of the year.

The Japanese Footbridge, 1899. The Philadelphia Museum of Art

When Monet was older, people finally started to appreciate his paintings. He settled down in the French town of Giverny, and built a wonderful water garden there.

Water Lilies, 1919-1926. Cleveland Museum of Art

Claude Monet lived to be 86 years old. He spent the last ten years of his life painting scenes of his water garden. These paintings are among the most beautiful and famous paintings he did. Some of them are over forty feet wide!

Panel of Water Lily Decorations, Musée d l'Orangerie, Paris Giraudon/Art Resource

Monet was able to show how things looked at the moment he saw them, almost like a camera does.

Snow at Argenteuil, Museum of Fine Arts, Boston

He loved nature and he painted with colors so that a scene would look as much like nature as possible. He was even able to paint mist and fog and make it look real.

Venice the Grand Canal, 1908. Museum of Fine Arts, Boston

It's a lot of fun to see a real Monet painting, especially up close. You'll be surprised by how many different colors you can see and how simple Monet's brush strokes are.

The paintings in this book came from the museums listed below. If none of these museums is close to your home, maybe you can visit one when you are on vacation.

The Art Institute of Chicago, Chicago, Illinois
Cleveland Museum of Art, Cleveland, Ohio
Louvre, Paris, France
The Metropolitan Museum of Art, New York, New York
Musée Marmottan, Paris, France
Musée d'l'Orangerie, Paris, France
Museum of Fine Arts, Boston, Massachusetts
The National Gallery of Art, Washington, D.C.
Neue Pinakothek, Munich, Germany
The Philadelphia Museum of Art, Philadelphia, Pennsylvania
Wadsworth Atheneum, Hartford, Connecticut

LEARN MORE BY TAKING THE
MONET QUIZ!

(ANSWERS ON THE NEXT PAGE.)

1. Why did Monet have a special studio boat built?
- ⓐ So he could water-ski and paint at the same time
- ⓑ Because he was tired of having his regular studio flood every time it rained
- ⓒ So he could travel easily up and down rivers and streams to paint his favorite scenes
- ⓓ Because he liked to challenge other artists to boat races

2. What is Etretat?
- ⓐ The name of Claude Monet's favorite French pastry
- ⓑ A coastal town in northern France with unusual rock formations that Monet loved to paint
- ⓒ The name of Monet's pet guinea pig

3. When things went wrong with one of his paintings, Claude Monet was known to have…
- ⓐ A mild reaction
- ⓑ A somewhat upset response
- ⓒ A really bad get-out-of-the-way-run-for-your-life outburst!

4. What were some of Claude Monet's favorite foods?
- ⓐ Roast duck, steamed chestnuts, ox-tail stew, and wild mushrooms
- ⓑ Fried water lilies
- ⓒ Tofu hot dogs

5. When Monet and his wife visited Paris, they liked to attend…
- ⓐ Concerts
- ⓑ The opera
- ⓒ Wrestling matches
- ⓓ All of the above

6. Claude Monet was one of four important artists who helped put together the first Impressionist show. The other three were…
- ⓐ David Crosby, Stephen Stills, and Graham Nash
- ⓑ Pierre Auguste Renoir, Alfred Sisley, and Camille Pissarro
- ⓒ Larry Fine, Moe Howard, and Curly Howard

ANSWERS

1. **c** Because water scenes were one of Monet's favorite subjects, he had a floating studio built. Another famous artist of the time, Edouard Manet, painted a picture of Claude Monet working on his floating studio. You can see this on page 7 of this book.

2. **b** Etretat is a town in in the Normandy region of France. Monet loved to paint the rocky cliffs and rough sea there.

3. **c** Claude Monet was known to throw a fit if he didn't like how his painting turned out. Sometimes an angry Monet would scrape all the paint off the canvas, or even throw the painting away!

4. **a** Claude Monet loved to eat but he was very fussy about how food was prepared. He especially enjoyed veggies from his own garden and fish from his pond.

5. **d** The Monets enjoyed all kinds of entertainment, including Mrs. Monet's favorite: wrestling matches!

6. **b** The Paris Salon judges rejected so many artists' paintings that Monet, Renoir, Sisley, and Pissarro decided to put on their own show. Thirty artists joined them in the first impressionist show in 1874.

HEY, WHAT DOES THAT WORD MEAN?

appreciate (uh-PREE-shee-ate) To enjoy or value somebody or something

canvas (KAN-vuhss) A surface for painting made from canvas cloth stretched over a wooden frame

conditions (kuhn-DISH-uhnz) The state of the weather at a given time

easel (EE-zuhl) A folding wooden stand used to support a painting

impressionism (im-PRESH-uh-niz-uhm) A style of painting invented in the late 1800s, in which the artist uses color and loose brushstrokes to capture a visual "impression" of the moment

model (MOD-uhl) Someone who poses for an artist

reflect (re-FLEKT) To act like a mirror

Salon (suh-LAHN) A yearly art exhibition in Paris that began in 1725; it was considered the greatest annual art event in Europe in the 1800s

studio (STOO-dee-oh) A room or building in which an artist works

Visit this Scholastic Web site for more information on Claude Monet:
www.factsfornow.scholastic.com
Enter the keywords **Claude Monet**

INDEX